Dedication

I've written this book of poems dedicated to cancer patients. I'd like to call them: survivors, everywhere. We are a select group, a strong group bonded by a disease that is mythical and profound. And incurable.

Yet, with a positive mental attitude, we can survive and flourish. It is incumbent upon us fighters to be an example of empathy, perseverance, and positivity. Keep fighting!

Amy —

Please enjoy this book. It's been such a pleasure to be your brother for these many years. Find a quiet place & have a good read. :)

"It is a test [that] genuine poetry can communicate before it is understood." — *T. S. Eliot, from the essay "Dante."*

Table of Contents

Dedication..1
Epigraph..2
Table of Contents...3-5
Preface..6-7
Acknowledgements..8
Introduction...9
Perfection...10
Bridge...11
Prescient..12
Moss...13
Withered..14
Places...15
Falling..16
Beautiful..17
Awnings...18
Subtle Nuances..19
Passed..20
Bluebonnet..22
Crash In Equal Proportions..22

Blind Corners 23

Spring's Doorway 24

Forgetting 25

My Lake 26

Salty 27

Waterfall 28

Brushstrokes and Echoes 29

Catacomb 30

Im(mortal) 31

Dimly Lit 32

Why 33

Dark Thicket 34

Painted Lady 35

Broken 36

Clean Through 37

Half 38

Drying Clothes 39

Grandmom 40

A Love We Can't Touch 41

Act 2 42

Inadvertent Friend 43-44

It's Time 45

Centrifugal..46

Ink...47

Fighting a Rolling Fog..48

Twisting a Frayed Rope...49

Elixir..50

Match...51

Virtue...52

Fear Comes Calling...53

Pieces of Fabric..54

Healer's Hand..55

Certain...56

Laundered..57

Windows...*58-59*

Angels..60-61

Epilogue..62

About The Author...63

Preface

Once you are diagnosed with Stage Four Cancer, there is such a demonstrative change in your psyche. Your mind races for mental relief. My source of relief came through a familiar exercise- writing poetry. It's a passion that has existed in me since the age of 8, when I wrote my first poem. Immediately, then, I came to love poetry as a means of expressing my inner romance of life.

Poetry seems the most improbable art form in the age of texting and abbreviations. The poetry that was letter-writing, seems destined to die and never return.

Here, an example of a Civil War letter from Union Officer Sullivan Ballou, to his spouse, written from the front lines.

My very dear Sarah: The indications are very strong that we shall move in a few days- perhaps tomorrow. Lest I should not be able to write again, I feel impelled to write a few lines that may fall under your eye when I shall be no more...

I have no misgivings about, or lack of confidence in the cause in which I am engaged, and my courage does not halt or falter. I know how strongly American Civilization now leans on the triumph of the Government and how great a debt we owe to those who went before us through the blood and sufferings of the Revolution. And I am willing- perfectly willing- to lay down all my joys in this life, to help maintain this Government, and to pay that debt...

Sarah my love for you is deathless, it seems to bind me with mighty cables that nothing but Omnipotence could break; and yet my love of this country comes over my like a strong wind and bears me unresistably on with all these chains to the battle field.

The memories of the blissful moments I have spent with you come creeping over me, and I feel most gratified to God and to you that I have enjoyed them for so long. And hard it is for me to give them up and burn to ashes the hopes of future years, when, God willing, we might still have lived and loved together, and seen our sons grown up to honorable manhood, around us. I have, I know, but few and small claims upon Divine Providence, but something whispers to me- perhaps it is the wafted prayer of my little Edgar, that I shall return to my loved ones unharmed. If I do not my dear Sarah, never forget how much I love you, and when my last breath escapes me on the battlefield, it will whisper your name. Forgive my many faults and the many pains I have caused you. How thoughtless and foolish I have often times been! How gladly would I wash out with my tears every little spot upon your happiness...

But, O Sarah! If the dead can come back to this earth and flit unseen around those they loved, I shall always be near you; in the gladdest days and in the darkest nights... always, always, and if there be a soft breeze upon your check, it shall be on my breath, as the cool air fans your throbbing temple, it shall be my spirit passing by. Sarah do not mourn me dead; think I am gone and wait for thee, for we shall meet again...

Sullivan died a week later. Will we ever see such beautiful writing again?

With the purchase of this book, I ask you to memorialize the artform of poetry. As I did with the above Union Officer, I would like for all poetry to henceforth be revered and shared. Thus, keeping the art, the words, and the spirit within alive.

Acknowledgements

I'd like to thank the following friends and family for their invaluable and honest criticism of my work. Poets tend to believe that their work is better than it actually is, so a panel of trusted readers is a must if you want a book that others might want to read.

So, it is that I thank the following:

Father Bruce Wren

Carol Burt

Nicole Binder

Introduction

There are few of my poems that can be ingested in one read. I've intentionally attempted to hide multiple meanings into each poem. Of course, the interpretation of an individual poem is reserved for the reader. What applies to one hopeful reader may well be entirely different to the other.

Perfection

Little to do,

To perfection I found

No tussling, adjusting, or like

Entirely unneeded – this touching up

Or making right – it was made that way

Right, in a way

I've now come to perfectly love

Recently - easily, this lack of criticism

That before – unreservedly spoiled

My waking words, my walking comments,

Compressed my lips and tongue

In distorted ugliness,

Spitting and spurting its own rejection

My angered imperfection – on no one,

Who didn't listen

Then,

With a tardy exclamation,

Perfection changed me

My temples sufficiently bleached,

And appreciation matured

Bridge

The chasm,

Covered,

For traveling hearts,

And many have passed upon

With haste

And with out

Most knew

Of the frailty here,

The gaping holes

More with haste

Than not

With a beat still

Healthy,

They fell,

To their end

And time,

Hadn't time,

To make repairs,

Whilst,

More slipped away

The bridge knows,

The count,

And it plainly bleeds

Prescient

An unnatural aura -

The halo you can't see

On the angel you won't admit

Or is it the things you can't touch?

It's the voodoo,

You can't trust -

The pinprick about your back,

You'll later deny

Until that singular moment

Stopped-

At the intersection of

Divinity and solemnity

The sun - high noon,

Bleeds a cross,

On your burning lawn

A tattered sod plot,

Where stones line up

Neatly, evenly,

Until you decide

Moss

There is moss on the limb,

And ants on that moss,

A frenetic, massive,

Familial reunion

Their communal choir,

Imperceptible to the ears,

Of local denizen,

They still chant

Darting all of one direction,

And again in none,

Crossing the oak limbs,

At odd right angles

The angstful tree, felled,

Snapped with a thunderous clap,

On a damp and electric evening,

After a biblical storm had passed

The clouds ranted,

Then coalesced,

Into a solid fist of fate

A silent vapor anvil

Softly landing on the forest floor

Upon a rush of winter leaves,

Her final repose announced

Exposing the cadre of Ants

Hidden within

On her side

Her age, too - revealed

Neat rings, tidy,

Each a year's flash,

An impregnable memory

Of repetitive seasons,

Wet - dry, warm – cold

Repeat

Withered

The shrill

Above the din,

An army of insistent angels,

Exhorting a cosmic,

If hysterical,

Harmony

Their voices - a mashing of everyone I've loved,

Or wished to

A single melodic affirmation,

A pitch,

Discernible by none other, than I

And I,

Needed, wanted, to be sung to –

And lifted

As the wind from under my wings,

Once inexhaustible,

Withered of late

Places

It's where we find ourselves,

In cornfields,

Amidst countless ears listening

Farming the earth for others

A city center,

Averting thousands of eyes,

Seeking to know more

On a vertical cliff

Clenched,

Ascending through fog,

Heavy in fear

It's the intersection of mortality,

Crossed with an earnest faith

We oblige these places,

With expectancy,

Abiding,

And simple hope

Did I claim this?

Comforting and maddening

At times, a mélange of both,

With no contemplation for the middle

A disquieting of,

Alternative endings

Falling

It's the falling...

The newborn arriving,

A calf birthing,

Received amidst

Incessant poverty,

Dusty, dried rations,

Over dark red water,

Douses the savannah,

Where the temple once stood

A shaman's exercise,

Mixed with an herbal epiphany,

"Believe in me,"

He said

And the dying obeyed,

Forgoing sanity

For a salty drop on the tongue,

Drained from dewy webs,

And cacti fingers

Beautiful

If not beautiful,

Then what?

If not perfect,

Then why?

And, if not timely,

Then when?

There is no answer quantifiable

Not otherwise extant

Just the awe of your

Birth

The halo of a God,

I see in your eyes,

And purity of soul

No works have yet been prescribed

For such an occasion

Awnings

A year,

And many,

Under the awnings of their eyes

Some lonely,

Others bleached to near fading

These pictures I hold,

Ominously devoid of color now,

Are just black and white

Stick figure parents,

Fashioning near gangster-long cars,

Sitting on white-walled tires,

Lining thin and long city streets,

Framed with tiny row homes

Poverty remnants,

Cheap plywood and Faux brick is all

They were all on the backside

Of an average life,

Shunning everything

that subtracted time

Subtle Nuances

There are subtle nuances,

In all human frailty

Bound, tied actually,

In an excruciating manner

Being poignant

Is to own the unbroken

As all in life

Inexplicably -

Is impoverished,

And undernourished

There is purity

In faith only,

And all primary colors

Yet, I can possess neither

I can subscribe to,

Be a paying member of,

But real goodness is too thin

To spread upon the unleavened

Passed

At her passing,

At her gravesite,

After decades of estrangement,

What prophecy can be brought

To this feast?

What celebration can't be recanted?

In a handbasket heavy,

Indecisive indecisions and

Ample remorse cripple

The shoulder they lay upon

There is agony

Causing an arduous leaning to the right,

Forcing me to walk in acerbic circles,

Around the fresh dirt

A primitive mound of fertile earth,

Placidly covering death

I pace,

Groping for a revelation,

That eases me into prayer.

I should be praying,

Right?

Bluebonnet

A rare time of rarer choosing,
That it might dominate my writing
About an evening in a Texas town,
Abrupt with filtered photos
Dry washed and tie-dyed,
All bleached with time, tears and,
Caliche dust

Still - and adhered,
Like vinyl film to a sun blistered,
And cracking picture window
Overlooking a searing service road,
Newly pressed with macadam,

The smell in my nose still permeates
Images and imprints,
Reserved for smiles thought remembered
Now soaking in a once proud sweat,
A love of the labor to survive

Crash in Equal Proportions

Skinny and deep,

And foreshadowed on the north,

Side of the pick or axe,

Or device that tacks me,

To an icy carapace

Crying in driblets that,

Hitting the bottom of the glass,

Clank and bounce and reflect,

The crowning sun through,

My misty heaving

Tethered anecdotally,

Until midday,

Or one day when,

The mountain exposes its inner angst,

And shakes me free

To crash the depth of my wanting,

Falling in equal proportions,

To my climb

Blind Corners

Where there is no light,

Exists a blind corner,

Springing into our middle-aged path

The omnipotent, all knowing,

Corrected path

The one that we sold

The passing of our youth to,

Exclaiming how it was truth,

clear and convergent

Our seminal certainty outlasted only by it's,

Newfound maturity

Lightly littered with righteousness

All too well – this unknown,

A calamitous void,

The deepest need unfilled,

…where am I going?

When is it too late,

To arrive

Spring's Doorway

It's fear and apathy,

That keeps me anchored

Just inches,

From Spring's open doorway

The halo it creates around,

My doorless frame

Boasts the warmth and hope,

Of Sun's bleeding

Inciting my nerves to action

I'd been so happy inside

It all appears – a postcard

Never mailed

A sudden throw from my kitchen table

Until the mailman walks in

Breaking the illusionary boundary,

Between hibernation,

And liberation

Forgetting

There is a subtle detachment,
From my limbs, lungs and loneliness
Now, being alone isn't new,
It's been my preferred state,
Of life, now and again
With a rather cyclical perversion

The limbs and lungs, though,
Well, they betray me
Sometimes ignore and hurt me,
While doing the simplest tasks
Routine chores, really

My memories are distant,
Like a high school sweetheart,
Who, coincidently, I recall- vividly
My sock drawer eludes me,
As does
My address and phone number,
But you're here

My Lake

My lake was angry today

Locked in a summer storm,

She threw wave after tempestuous wave,

Onto a beaten and tired shore

And with her misty wind,

She sang a raging opera,

Randomly bel canto

Then suddenly contralto,

Which gave me a blinding pause

Should I hear her siren through,

And brave the night, cozy beside her

Listen to her – completely,

Just this once

Will she sing me a tale,

Of good men in fine ships taken?

Or the smiles of children?

On their first sail?

Need I worry, that by listening

I'd have sealed my fate with her

Will my next cool midnight dip be my last?

Or will this God situated sea spare me,

Teach me,

And let me know the reflection,

Of sailors and children and low shooting stars?

In her black cape again,

Does she know that I fear her?

Or that I admire her?

Does she care?

Salty

The thick and particled salt air,
Refreshed all that I hoped it would
With wave upon wave,
Of near digital quality memories

The pier, the sand, the whistle at noon,
And the loneliness found in a large crowd
Adrift in conversations wafting by
Small tabloid talk mostly
Happy as a pigeon that these rumors,
Though vexing – belonged not to me

Surf left behind,
She made no sound

We agreed, we're tired,
Of strangers flouncing,
On our tide

My problems simultaneously easier and infinitely,
More distant - too far to be seen from shore
Saddened, I looked up and found the beach empty,
And quiet – again

Reconnecting with the pier, the sand,
And the whistle that blew at noon,
The waves slowed and winter approached,
Kneeling on the eroded fragments of the

Waterfall

One smile at a time,

In different ways,

And at different times,

I lost myself

The roadmap blurred – watered down,

By tears on loan,

From memories yet encumbered,

Upon my heaving chest

Coyly, I dropped crumbs,

To remind and find,

Only to watch them,

In day-night rearview mirrors,

Swept upstream

And hope – as hard to hold,

As the waterfall,

I find myself under – soaked,

With every intention,

To wring sunlight from it

Brushstrokes and Echoes

Scars -

Brushstrokes and echoes,

In sinewy landscapes,

Laid bare on canvas

Paint drying,

In mid drip,

torrents of tears,

In oil captured

Her admission,

A blurry bio,

Of things best not seen,

Pain best not felt

And if I could focus,

There – beauty would be,

Where it's meant to reside

But not from the painter's view,

Only from her dulcet palette

Catacomb

The damp walls,

Sweat-full with ancient toils

Bending and bowing,

Under the weight,

Of such greatness

A hall of what was right

The crystal sconces,

chingle and change,

On every gape,

Of dead breath coming from-

The catacombs

A chamber of old, cold and,

Recumbent bones,

That sit, skinless,

Faceless,

Pointing at each other

Fixed in a permanent stare,

Without a care left,

To exhume

Im(mortal)

With no effort I admit,

My mortality

All at once perverse and perfect,

In its reluctance to be blushed

Only my thoughts, above it

Immortal – my dreams substantial

Clever in the detail – remembering colors,

And objects and sentences

And that song –

Played intermittently but interminably,

Revisiting me awake and asleep

Touching and teasing me,

That – you were there – certainly

Dimly Lit

Orange embers,

From my filter-less cigarette,

Glow brighter still,

Through the cloud of smoke,

Pouring into the room

Otherwise it's dark

And damp

The weather won't cooperate,

With my sullen mood

And my eyes burn from the,

now prolonged life of,

My daily wear contacts

And it's Monday – for Christ's sake

So, I drag on the cigarette again,

Oddly comforted by the crackling,

Of the dry tobacco

And the momentary flash of light,

It has caused

Why

The word "why" decries me

Berates me,

In excruciating doubt,

Of what is faith and above

And robs me of options

It separates me,

From my foundation,

And worries me that,

There'll be no end,

To the question,

Whether here or beyond

I'm scratching the inside of my

Brain

Scrubbing every memory

Every smell touch and sound,

To find the wrong path I took,

To bring me here,

At the crucible,

Of life

And your death

Dark Thicket

The dark thicket of trees,

And knee-high switchgrass,

Behind me,

Sing an eerie song of summer

An urgent admission of nature's,

Desire to see me leave

Each sound a different tenor

Each growing louder and more profuse

Flat footing it against a rising gradient

Dense clouds of prickly heat,

Gnaw at my fabric free neckline

And swarms of gnats enjoy the taste,

Of my skinny ankles

With more than one thought of mortality,

Consuming each desperate stumble

An error is committed – and I stop

I'll agree to meet this angry ensemble,

Bent over, hopelessly heaving,

A painful reminder,

That I've acquiesced

Compelled to apologize for the ragged,

Encroachment of man,

I scream a pathetic apology,

Citing our good intentions,

Our Foolishness,

And neglect

The wind blows a message,

Pushing me back to the grandstands

Where I'll wait – in solemn agreement

It's too late she said,

It's too late

Painted Lady

So, I've taken advantage,
Of a painted lady,
On a sweltering,
Summer night

I'll admit I didn't,
Last as long as I should have
A shrunken violet,
I'm not – but...

But proud – if, at this moment,
One can easily claim it,
Profoundly or otherwise
I just laughed as I stumbled,
Down to stairs

To the curb,
Into the car,
Racing back,
With a rancid heart,
To a more normal,
Placid place

Broken

Everything,

The sun to cherish you,

An angel to walk with you,

A cloudless trail for miles,

Before you

Is it fair to still be – broken,

With no repayment plan,

And no remorse,

Just sadness and a mirror

Would a single note on a baby grand?

Still please you?

An empty easel,

Make you yearn – for the beauty yet,

Envisioned there

A Mona Lisa smile,

With your name on it

Can you have everything,

And nothing at all?

Or the everything you have,

… everything you have.

Clean through

She tends the wound,
The whole clean through
Touching everything,
Inside the man

This man...
Gasps for air
Convulses a "thank you",
For her gentleness,
And warm hands

Fluttering eyes,
Now,
Ardently fixed upon her

He knows,
And too - she knows
A year now,
She tends this man's grave,
Touching everything,
That was the man

A John Doe lover,
Below her feet

Half

Half of me,

For the whole of you

A fraction, unbecoming,

An - unwelcome proportion

And I try,

To shift to the giving,

Put more in

But for an invisible,

Elastic sense,

Of self worth

A living echo,

Dividing my virtue,

From my fault

Amplifying,

A smoldering soul

Drying Clothes

Pregnant pillowcases,

Slapping the tense twine,

Between an agitated slanted porch,

And a hazy labored horizon

Filling and exhaling – but,

Drying patiently – wrinkle free,

From summer's warm breathing,

And evening's cool intentioned breezes

A fall season is pending,

In the brown and bending wheat,

An acre or two away

Long sleeved shirts,

Shoved into apparent applause

Celebrate a tangled and tied unison,

Adding to the season's cacophony

The evergreens moan,
Seeing no pleasure

And yet, no remorse,

In the changing weather

Stout and green with celery stalk strength,

They've been here before

Grandmom

It's the ocean that I recall, mostly
The mist it created before the burning noon sun
And the soothing ocean sound – that put us to sleep,
In two tiny cots, each June or July

We were at our brightest and most loving there,
9th Avenue, in the middle of the block
The clanking of a bicycle chain,
Foretold the sunup ride of Grandpop
On his, then ancient, Schwinn,
And how I wished to go along

I haven't had melba toast since,
I've not powdered anyone's feet since,
Nor has anyone said the work "again" – the same way again
Nor would I want them to
These were your signature on my soul- indelible
Nor could a few poetic words capture,
All the love you gave, selflessly,
Freely,
With no barriers, no remorse

A Love we can't touch

A child met God,

Upon her heart stopping,

On a cold table, in a strange city

When the surgeon said – "now".

She ascended …

And for a time was taught,

About purity ,

And love,

Faith and grace,

Forgiveness and acceptance,

And things we don't yet know

But she now knows

He coddled and kissed her,

Whispered,

"I Love You"

And sent her on her way,

Back to her parents - waiting

Full of an understanding,

We can't know -

A love we can't yet touch

She spent a short time in eternity

And came home an Angel

ACT 2

Can I convince you,

Cajole you – ask you to

Believe?

Persuade you,

With gifts, like,

Love and kindness

For money, I don't possess

Would that alarm you?

As none have yet been,

Shall I say, consistent

Short of begging,

Acts surpass rhetoric,

I've heard

So, act I must,

And believe you might,

That sharing and caring,

Trumps words and blustering

Inadvertent friend

A friend, new and abrupt,

Has found me

No casual acquaintance this,

Rather the deliberate long-term kind,

Alit with measurable angst

Neither the marrying type,

Though brusquely

Betrothed we now are,

Sharing a familial permanence

We live in silent detente

A cold war of denial and aggression,

Whose disadvantage belongs – solely, sadly

To me.

She's been awakened,

By my very weakness,

And myriad bad habits

Compounded by choices of risk – my personal brand,

That seemed neither sinister nor toxic – then

I brood - she plots

Sadistically dormant,

These many good and loving years,

No inkling nor whisper of the harassment to follow

My faith now drawn, a solemn ancient sword,

Kept closely in reserve,

Procured and confirmed

For this restlessness, this eventfulness

It's all I have, for she's burrowed so deeply,

That the poison aimed to demise me

Now resides within me – a soupçon of distasteful evil

More time with hands clasped,

Might excise her sinewy grip, but,

Confoundedly I've not sought out,

The right amount of crying,

For the right amount of dying

Its Time

Now just a photo,

In a frame

A sad and dusty reminder

A tragic snapshot in time

A time when there was,

So much of it left

We couldn't know,

Then,

That one of us would,

Quit

Quit living,

And loving,

Quit promising,

And hoping

I'll keep it out,

Of the sun's focus,

As to not fade

I'd just die again,

If the color in your eyes,

Vanished again

Centrifugal

It's the perfect first line,
The opening
A directed salvo of painful predilection,
Meant to humble you,
Guilt you,
Surface you with all ballasts,
Screaming freedom

It's a cry for a "look at me",
A two-faced mirror,
Looking convexly then covertly
Cajoling, intimating,
That my words should be,
Your words

We should feel the same,
Soulmate affliction
As anything less, I tell you,
Couldn't be destiny,
Can't be ordained

It's the crisp edges of,
The corners of,
This side of- romance
Where all ends meet,
Squarely in the middle,
Roundly objectified,
But I'll rationalize

Despite my spinning it,
Tearing and tumbling it,
You'll get it
You were meant to,
Get it

Ink

Ink drops,

Poison blood,

For a brooding poet

Because,

All poets brood

And bleed,

Thoughts, laments

Some minor,

Most major

The pen,

Trembling,

The words - sure

Fighting a Rolling Fog

At morning's rise, an hour earlier,
Than I'm used to waking,
Came a fog, calling

In waves, from the lake's door,
She knocked,
And kept knocking,
Until

There was room in my view,
To see her
A home in my heart,
To greet her

From which we both knew,
That my arms couldn't hold her
And her lips couldn't kiss me,
But no less was the,
Beauty in her coming

Twisting a frayed rope

Your life is twisted,

In impossible ways

A thin frayed rope,

Curled tight by,

Regret and delight,

Love, lust, and loss

Particularly,

For the pleasure of,

No one

This intimate tale,

Of you

Is the cross you'll bear

Whose weight will,

On one seminal day,

Fell you – completing,

Your unknown and untold,

Journey

Until history makes it so

Elixir

The sustenance of crazy,
To do crazy things,
While slim on excuses,
It's tendered, or not willing

Until there is no subtlety,
Remaining
But wanton direction,
And perilous trails to traverse

Many are new,
Even novel,
Until they lead,
To the spray of a waterfall

The downspout of,
Anxious events,
Lying, waiting,
For you to jump

… in
Or down
Through the mist,
And the fight,
A crucible and a lake,
Of floating, Indiscernible,
Thoughts

Tide and timing,
Comes the splash
A wakeful reminder,
That all is expendable,
But mercifully reversible too

Match

A simple match,

Lit a fire,

Lit a conversation,

That stays alight,

In darkness,

Damp or cold

A trivial flame –

Smoldering,

Until her meaning,

Comes – and her,

Shadow revealed

No instant blaze

This – took time,

And fanning

The gentle breeze,

Of love,

Now a storm,

Irrevocable, beguiled,

Replete with a murmured hum,

A breathful whisper,

The hush of a satisfied journey

Virtue

Where is virtue,

When beauty lies,

And dying is glamorized and commoditized?

When fish can't spawn,

And dignity can't roost,

Where a kiss is a sendoff,

An embrace, a flirtation

When ice melts,

And our conscience sinks,

Because global warming is not an emotion

Where self-effacing,

Is self-explanatory

Where – I'm sorry is followed by,

"I didn't"

When a language is cauterized,

To fit the lyrics,

And – I love you,

Is conveniently past tense

Why the elders can't remember,

What the youth can't forget

For a falling leaf – is raked,

Not planted

Where alone – is preferred

And poetry?

My beloved poetry –

Is a postscript to a romantic life

Fear Comes Calling

In the largess of her guises,

She'll come calling, fear,

Inopportunely, sardonically,

And uniquely,

A sound known only,

To you

Lurking in a shadow,

You can't yet light

With bravado shattered,

She'll dance about your shards,

Left scattered and upright,

Like glass in the desert

Lightning kissed sand,

You might stammer and scream,

But its only,

An echo in a vacuum

Surely,

You'll need faith,

And more kneeling,

To keep her quiet

Pieces of Fabric

Silk, we were,
Frictionless,
Two pieces of fabric,
Gliding together

At times
One,
In a bundle,
An indiscernible ball

The same color,
Same dye ,
But older, one,
The other younger

Time had her way,
Void of any emotion,
She let vivid colors fade,
Unevenly

Differences emerged
Perhaps the grass,
Wasn't greener,
From a distance

Or that fading was,
A better option than,
Disappearing entirely

Healer's Hands

Calloused and chaffed,

The bracteolate hands of the healer

Careworn and dusty from reddish brown earth,

Currently matting the clumped hair,

Above his sun-pinked ears

Spitting on them, to loosen,

The small parts of the ground,

He now permanently carried

From alter to pew,

Sinner to saint

Church and home again –

(Wherever home took him)

Unaware that the cracking flesh,

Separated in places, where creases formed,

And maroon blood flowed,

Upon the ground, wherever his work's hardship was borne,

Creating perfect circles

In the vastness of this ocean of land

Certain

There isn't a haze,

Nor foggy bog

No place free for the,

Wondering

It's meant -

In a way that,

Resolute invented,

Where hard,

Isn't granite enough

And

Doubt is ignored at peril's prodding,

Persistent though she is

You know,

That you know

Despite your,

Wispy ignorance,

It's certain

Laundered

I've laundered you,
Haven't I?
Cleansed the very personality,
From your vibrancy
Unwittingly perhaps,
But with no small measure,
Of control

Tugging the smile, the sound of,
Your voice,
And the tenor of your soul,
To make myself whole

I've mined you,
Stripped from you,
Not gleefully,
But mandatorily

You were,
contemptuously,
Beautiful,
Alarmingly so

And I wanted it,
Required it,

Married it
Then marred it all to say,
That you were-
Mine

Windows

They are, it's said,

The windows to our souls,

And how envious

To be able to search so vast,

A number

Are you surprised by their prescience?

And their goodness,

Their discontent or favor?

Can you see God – where others can't,

Or dreams unfinished?

Or regret, heaped like banana leaves,

On a vast beach – where the water is,

Blue and green – lapping the sand,

Like your mothers gentle hand

Do they all flirt with you – with the hope,

Of a clearer vision,

Or hindsight – lamentably

Are you frightened to see,

The beginning of the end,

Of a life as sweet as Vermont molasses?

When the lights are flickering,

And no one cares

Or is it the past you see – like a fine,

Documentary,

Revealing what was once good

And will be again?

Angels

The angels you earn,
Aren't like those in your dreams
They arrive quietly, softly,
Around the fringes of your life
Courteously whispering their intentions

In the beginning, they require care
Not unlike new flowers, in your garden,
In Spring – talking to them helps

They don't float, nor wear white,
At least not initially
They visit – opportunely
Never extend their purpose –
I suppose they don't always know

They don't evaporate when you try,
To hold them, or kiss them
Some kiss you back, as early as a year,
And learn your name –
depending on you to recognize it

Most resemble you – or some part of you:

Your ears – perhaps

And your mother reminded you that,

You'd have one of your own,

And they'd be a handful

So be careful what you ask for

In your care they reward you

The more you love, the more they love

In their eyes, so are you

And we name them, the prettiest name,

We can find, praying they agree too

But they never will

And so it goes, that these angels,

Inadvertently bless us, simply by breathing,

Or by reaching out – on a brilliant day,

And say – Dadda

Epilogue

I'll keep writing poetry as long as God allows. By now you realize that many of my poems are rooted in faith.

You've probably also now realized that all periods are missing from where they belong in every verse. Periods symbolize the end, whereas my poetry indicates the exact opposite. So, it is I have excluded that punctuation. Question marks, dashes, colons, commas, semicolons, and suspension points indicate continuation. For that reason, they can be found throughout my writing.

Further, the lack thereof allows the reader to decipher their own meaning or translation, which good poetry should espouse.

About the author

Born in Philadelphia, Pennsylvania, in the year of 1960, Paul J. Burt experienced everything from the Civil Rights Movement to the assassination of a President. He sat and watched Neal Armstrong step foo on the moon and the Vietnam war come to an end. These early experiences undoubtedly formed a basis for Paul's writing.

From there, life evolved into a series of fortunate events that inspired and delighted him... Until the summer of 2016 when he learned he had Stage Four Thyroid Cancer. It was at that moment that he realized that if he wanted to share his writing, he would need to do so with Godspeed.

This, and future books, encapsulate both the highs and lows of such a disease. Fear gives way to hope and hope translates to faith.

Paul is married to Janet and has four children: Brian, Erica, Sophia, and Hudson. He lives in Lake Forest, Illinois. A constant tinkerer of the written word, he also loves to collect and restore vintage automobiles.